_ □ X

CODING
WITH
VIDEO GAMES

BY KYLIE BURNS

Express!

BELLWETHER MEDIA • MINNEAPOLIS, MN

T0018754

Imagination comes alive in Express! Transform the everyday into the fresh and new, discover ways to stir up flavor and excitement, and experiment with new ideas and materials. Express! makerspace books: where your next creative adventure begins!

This edition first published in 2024 by Bellwether Media, Inc.

No part of this publication may be reproduced in whole or in part without written permission of the publisher. For information regarding permission, write to Bellwether Media, Inc., Attention: Permissions Department, 6012 Blue Circle Drive, Minnetonka, MN 55343.

Library of Congress Cataloging-in-Publication Data

Names: Burns, Kylie, author.
Title: Coding with video games / by Kylie Burns.
Description: Minneapolis, MN : Bellwether Media, 2024. | Series: Express! Adventures in unplugged coding |
  Includes bibliographical references and index. | Audience: Ages 7-13 | Audience: Grades 4-6 | Summary:
  "Information accompanies instructions for various video-game-themed activities that demonstrate skills needed
  for coding. The text level and subject matter are intended for students in grades 3 through 8"-- Provided by publisher.
Identifiers: LCCN 2023022000 (print) | LCCN 2023022001 (ebook) | ISBN 9798886875195 (library binding) |
  ISBN 9798886875690 (paperback) | ISBN 9798886877076 (ebook)
Subjects: LCSH: Computer programming--Juvenile literature. | Video games--Design--Juvenile literature.
Classification: LCC QA76.76.V54 B87 2024 (print) | LCC QA76.76.V54 (ebook) | DDC 005.13--dc23/eng/20230602
LC record available at https://lccn.loc.gov/2023022000
LC ebook record available at https://lccn.loc.gov/2023022001

Text copyright © 2024 by Bellwether Media, Inc. EXPRESS and associated logos are trademarks and/or registered trademarks of Bellwether Media, Inc.

Editors: Sarah Eason and Christina Leaf
Illustrator: Eric Smith
Series Design: Brittany McIntosh
Graphic Designer: Paul Myerscough

Printed in the United States of America, North Mankato, MN.

TABLE OF CONTENTS _ □ X

WHAT IS UNPLUGGED CODING? _ □ X

Coding is an awesome tool that people called programmers, or coders, use to talk to computers. It allows them to **communicate** instructions to a computer in its own language. Coders write **commands** known as **code** to give computers instructions.

Every video game begins with coders and code.

Unplugged coding is coding without a computer! Like coding with a computer, unplugged coding involves following step-by-step instructions. In this book, you will learn coding skills such as problem-solving and **decomposition** through activities that do not use a single piece of technology. To make it even more fun, we will use video games as our theme!

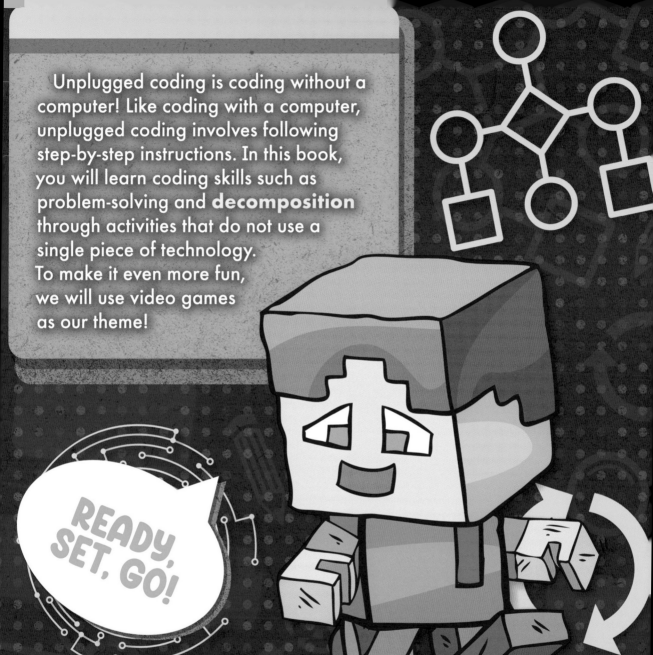

READY, SET, GO!

ESCAPE FROM THE MUMMY! _ □ X

Solving problems is an important part of coding. When coders find errors in a code, they use many skills to fix them. First, they must understand what went wrong. Then, they must come up with a step-by-step plan to fix the problem. Finally, those steps are written into the code.

In this activity, imagine that you are a treasure hunter in a video game. You are locked in a tomb with a sleeping mummy! You find a priceless treasure but cannot find a way out. Use problem-solving to find a way to escape before the mummy wakes up!

LET'S TRY IT OUT!

1

You use your flashlight to look around the tomb and spot a scroll sticking out of a jar. You take it out and unroll it. One side of the scroll has a chart with images and letters.

2

On the back of the scroll, you see a riddle. It is written as a code using a series of images from the chart on the front of the scroll. It may hold the secret to escaping!

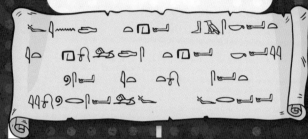

3

Using the chart, decode the message and record it with your pencil and paper. Follow the instructions and see what happens!

TURN THE PAGE TO SEE HOW YOU DID!

DID YOU KNOW?

Just like coders, the ancient Egyptians used codes to communicate. They were picture words called hieroglyphs.

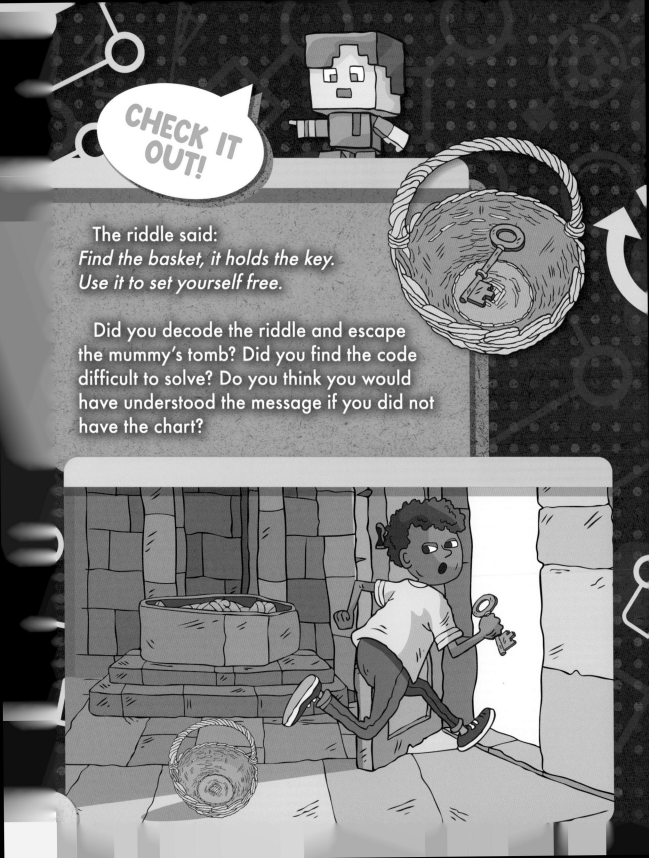

CHECK IT OUT!

The riddle said:
Find the basket, it holds the key.
Use it to set yourself free.

Did you decode the riddle and escape the mummy's tomb? Did you find the code difficult to solve? Do you think you would have understood the message if you did not have the chart?

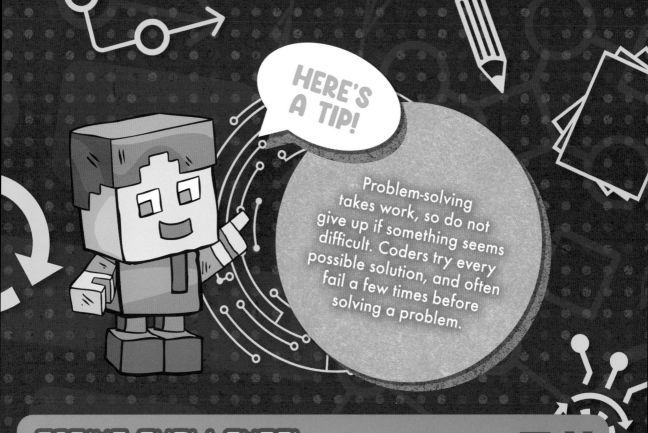

HERE'S A TIP!

Problem-solving takes work, so do not give up if something seems difficult. Coders try every possible solution, and often fail a few times before solving a problem.

CODING CHALLENGE!   _ □ X

You Will Need:
- a large ball of yarn
- masking tape
- a large room or outdoor space

Try this laser maze problem-solving game with some friends. Tape one end of the yarn to a door handle or chair. Then, zigzag the yarn across the space to create a maze. The yarn will be the lasers. Everyone begins with 10 points. The goal is to make it through the maze one at a time without touching the yarn. Players can step over or crawl under the yarn, but they cannot touch it. If they do, they have been zapped and lose 10 points! If they make it across without touching the yarn, they gain 10 points. The player with the highest score after five turns wins!

9

DOG PUZZLE
_ □ X

Have you ever had a big problem to solve? Sometimes coders run into problems when they write the code for a video game. When that happens, they look at what the end result should be and work backward to achieve the goal. This is called decomposition.

In this activity, imagine that you are designing a video game character. Use decomposition and problem-solving to help you make it!

GAME ON!

Study the picture of the completed dog below.

2

Think about the order of the steps needed to create the dog's face as shown in the picture.

3

Look at the origami step images below. Decompose the problem by looking at the pictures that are out of order.

4

Start with your square of paper, and then fold it following the order of steps you think is correct.

DID YOU KNOW?

Video game designers start creating a game by making detailed plans called storyboards. They include characters, stories, settings, and actions. The storyboard is turned into code.

TURN THE PAGE TO SEE HOW YOU DID!

CHECK IT OUT!

Below is the correct order the steps need to be in to complete the dog character. How did your dog character turn out? Was it difficult to create? Did you find it helpful to see the completed dog before you decomposed the steps?

HERE'S A TIP!

CODING CHALLENGE!

_ ▢ **X**

Try this decomposition activity with some friends. The problem is how to get the asteroids from one place to another, following the game rules.

You Will Need:
- 3 to 4 friends
- a cardboard box, filled with 8 to 10 balls that will be the asteroids
- an empty cardboard box, placed in another room
- a timer

You and your friends are astronauts in a video game. Your goal is to protect Earth from being destroyed by asteroids by sending them to a distant galaxy. Your mission is to move all of the asteroids to the empty box in the quickest way possible. Below are the rules:

1. Only one asteroid can be moved at a time.
2. You can walk but not run.
3. You may pass or toss an asteroid to another person.
4. If an asteroid is dropped, it must go back into the first box.
5. You have 60 seconds to complete your mission.

Start the timer and GO!

Programmers use a **loop** if they want the computer to repeat a specific action until a certain **condition** is met. The loop shortens the code because it removes the need to repeat the same command many times. Video games contain a core loop, which is the series of actions that a character repeats the most often. In this activity, you will use loops to complete a fun obstacle course!

- a hula hoop
- a bucket
- a limbo pole and stand
- a golf ball
- a golf putter
- a spoon
- an egg
- a die

LET'S GO!

DID YOU KNOW?

Video game programmers often create more than one loop when they code a game. This allows many actions to take place at the same time, just like in real life.

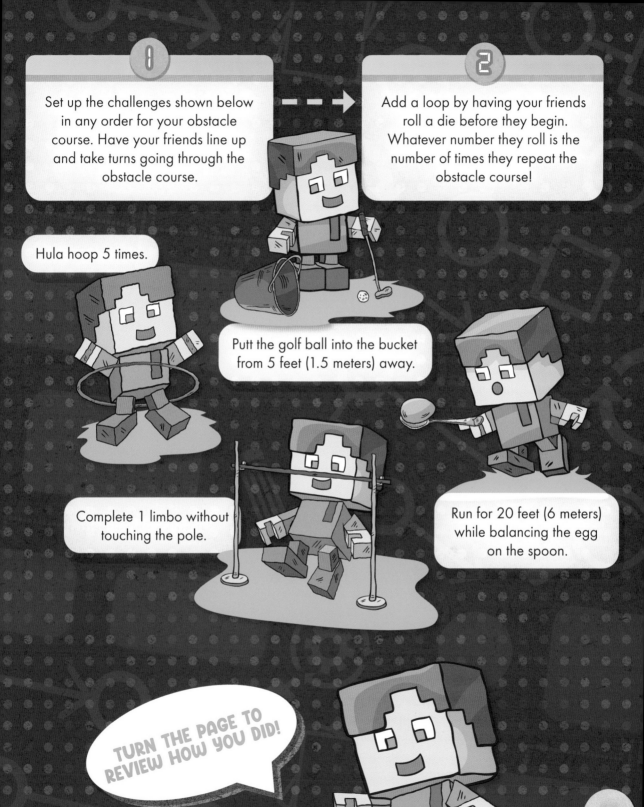

1

Set up the challenges shown below in any order for your obstacle course. Have your friends line up and take turns going through the obstacle course.

2

Add a loop by having your friends roll a die before they begin. Whatever number they roll is the number of times they repeat the obstacle course!

Hula hoop 5 times.

Putt the golf ball into the bucket from 5 feet (1.5 meters) away.

Complete 1 limbo without touching the pole.

Run for 20 feet (6 meters) while balancing the egg on the spoon.

TURN THE PAGE TO REVIEW HOW YOU DID!

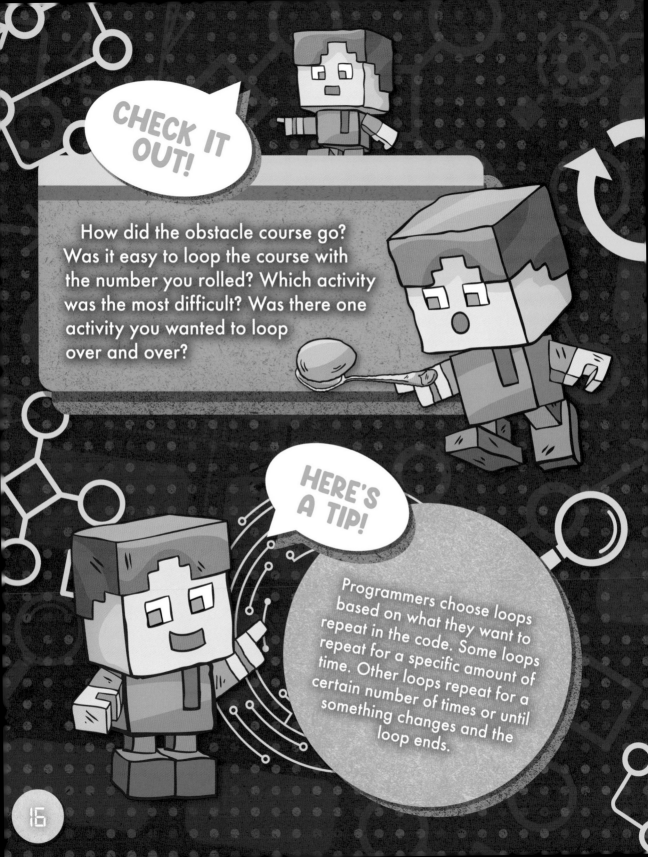

How did the obstacle course go? Was it easy to loop the course with the number you rolled? Which activity was the most difficult? Was there one activity you wanted to loop over and over?

HERE'S A TIP!

Programmers choose loops based on what they want to repeat in the code. Some loops repeat for a specific amount of time. Other loops repeat for a certain number of times or until something changes and the loop ends.

CODING CHALLENGE!

_ □ X

Come up with your own obstacle course with items you can find around your home. Some suggestions are shown below, but get creative with what you find! Make an activity for each set of objects. These will be your stations. Place the stations in a large circle. Have each person begin at a different activity and move in a repeating loop. Maybe add some levels of difficulty, such as singing a song while you go through the stations. When the song ends, so does the loop.

Throw 5 balls into a bucket from 5 feet (1.5 meters) away.

Jump rope for 1 minute without stopping.

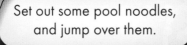

Set out some pool noodles, and jump over them.

Juggle bean bags for 30 seconds.

Video game design is complicated because the code must include many different possible **outcomes**. Each command is written in the game code. Programmers use **variables** to help organize information in the code. A variable is like a storage container that has many possible **values**. For example, a variable could be character actions, while the values could be running and jumping.

In this maze video game, fruits are the values! Choose a variable, or path, that you think will get you the most points with its values. One path has a hidden value behind the door at the end. Which will you choose?

LET'S PLAY!

1

Examine the maze carefully, looking at all of the paths.

2

Choose the path that you think will be the best route.

3

Using your finger, trace the path through the maze, collecting points along the way. Use your pencil and paper to add up your points as you go. What will you discover behind the door at the end of the maze?

Path A   Path B   Path C

TURN THE PAGE TO SEE BEHIND THE DOORS!

Check out the paths and the doors below. How did you decide on a path? Did the values that were represented by the fruits along each path affect your choice? How many points did you earn? Did you win the game and find the correct path to the prize or was there a ghost behind the door?

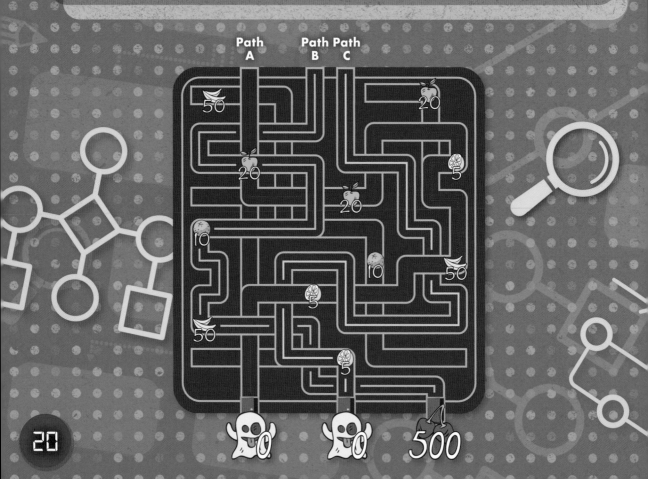

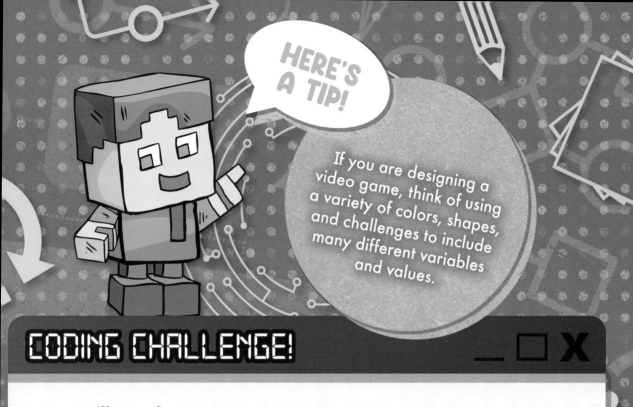

HERE'S A TIP!

If you are designing a video game, think of using a variety of colors, shapes, and challenges to include many different variables and values.

CODING CHALLENGE! _ □ X

You Will Need:
- a flat surface such as a driveway or sidewalk
- sidewalk chalk
- imagination!

If you were a video game designer, what type of maze would you create? Head outside with some sidewalk chalk, and create your own maze with variables. Can you think of a different theme for your game? How about an underwater theme or a jungle theme? What variables will you use? What values will you choose for the variables? When you have finished designing your maze, try it out with some friends.

I HOPE YOU ENJOYED UNPLUGGED CODING!

code—instructions for a computer

commands—specific instructions to complete a task

communicate—to share knowledge or information

condition—something that must occur before another action takes place

decomposition—the process of breaking down a problem or system into smaller parts

loop—a group of code that can be easily repeated

outcomes—results

values—pieces of information in a code; values are often part of a variable.

variables—parts of a code that store information; variables contain related values.

AT THE LIBRARY

McCue, Camille. *Getting Started with Coding: Get Creative with Code!* Indianapolis, Ind.: John Wiley and Sons, 2019.

Neuenfeldt, Elizabeth. *Video Games.* Minneapolis, Minn.: Bellwether Media, 2023.

Prottsman, Kiki. *How to Be a Coder.* New York, N.Y.: DK Publishing, 2019.

ON THE WEB

FACTSURFER

Factsurfer.com gives you a safe, fun way to find more information.

1. Go to www.factsurfer.com.

2. Enter "coding with video games" into the search box and click 🔍.

3. Select your book cover to see a list of related content.